THE PRIVATE
PRODUCTION OF
DEFENSE

THE PRIVATE PRODUCTION OF DEFENSE

—— by ——

Hans-Hermann Hoppe

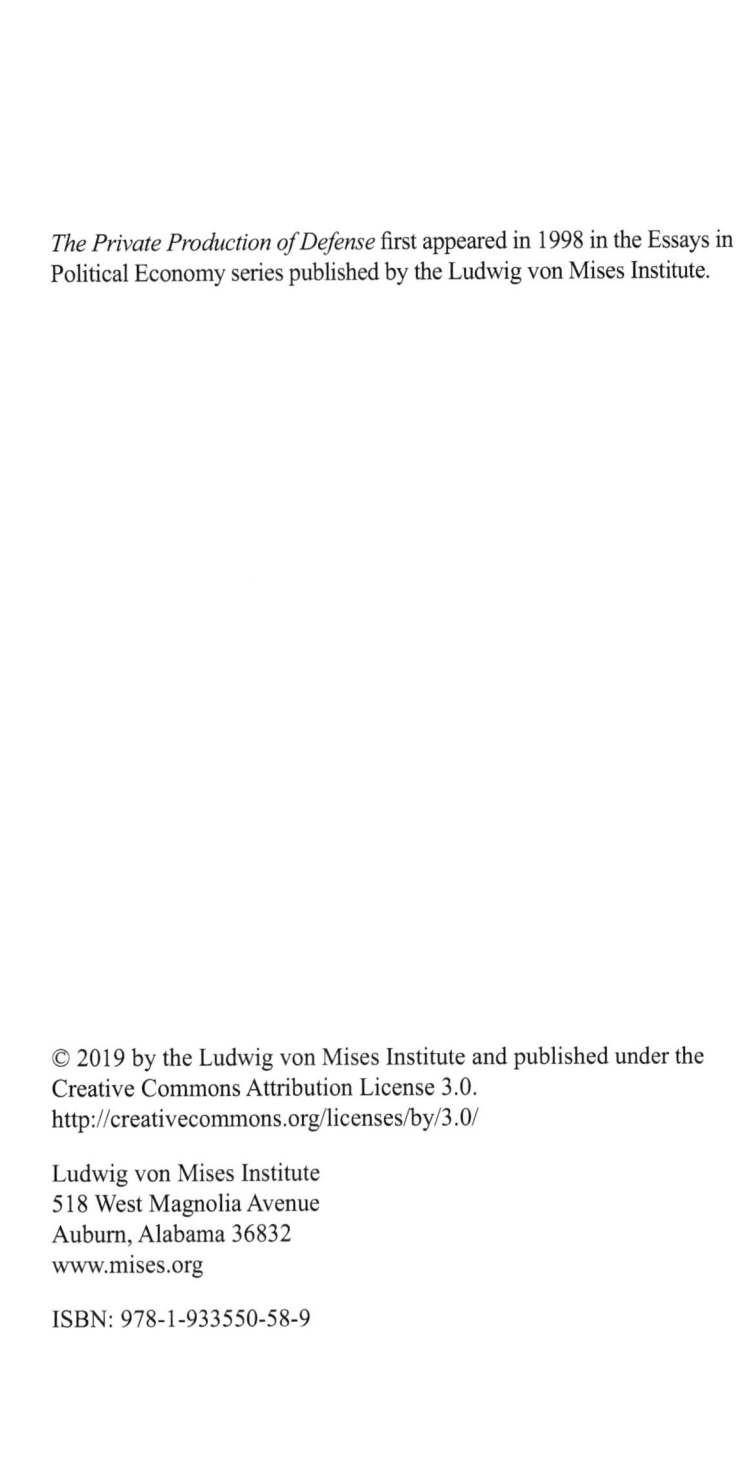

The Private Production of Defense first appeared in 1998 in the Essays in Political Economy series published by the Ludwig von Mises Institute.

© 2019 by the Ludwig von Mises Institute and published under the Creative Commons Attribution License 3.0.
http://creativecommons.org/licenses/by/3.0/

Ludwig von Mises Institute
518 West Magnolia Avenue
Auburn, Alabama 36832
www.mises.org

ISBN: 978-1-933550-58-9

Contents

SECTION ONE
The Private Production of Defense 7

SECTION TWO
The Empirical Evidence 13

SECTION THREE
How to Think About the Statist Response. 17

SECTION FOUR
The Case for Private Security 21

SECTION FIVE
More on Aggression Insurance 27

SECTION SIX
Political Borders and Insurance. 31

SECTION SEVEN
The Democratic State and Total War. 35

SECTION EIGHT
Insurance and Incentives 39

SECTION NINE
Insuring Against State Aggression 47

SECTION TEN
Regaining Our Right to Self-Defense 51

REFERENCES 53

1. The Private Production of Defense

AMONG THE MOST POPULAR AND CONSEQUENTIAL BELIEFS OF OUR age is the belief in collective security. Nothing less significant than the legitimacy of the modern state rests on this belief.

I will demonstrate that the idea of collective security is a myth that provides no justification for the modern state, and that all security is and must be private. Yet, before coming to the conclusion let me begin with the problem. First, I will present a two-step reconstruction of the myth of collective security, and at each step raise a few theoretical concerns.

The myth of collective security can also be called the Hobbesian myth. Thomas Hobbes, and countless political philosophers and economists after him, argued that in the state of nature, men would constantly be at each others' throats. *Homo homini lupus est*. Put in modern jargon, in the state of nature a permanent underproduction of security would prevail. Each individual, left to his own devices and provisions, would spend too little on his own defense, and hence, permanent interpersonal warfare would result. The solution to this presumably intolerable situation, according to Hobbes and his followers, is the institution of a state. In order to institute peaceful cooperation among themselves, two individuals, A and B, require a third independent party, S, as ultimate judge and peacemaker. However, this third party, S, is not just another individual, and the good provided by S, that of security, is not just another "private" good. Rather, S is a *sovereign* and has as such two unique powers. On the one hand, S can insist that his *subjects*, A and B, not seek protection from anyone but him; that is, S is a compulsory territorial monopolist of protection. On the other hand, S can determine unilaterally how much A and B must spend on their own security; that is, S has the power to impose taxes in order to provide security "collectively."

In commenting on this argument, there is little use in quarreling over whether man is as bad and wolf-like as Hobbes supposes, except to note that Hobbes's thesis obviously cannot mean that man is driven only and exclusively by aggressive instincts. If this were the case, mankind would have died out long ago. The fact that he did not demonstrates that man also possesses reason and is capable of constraining his natural impulses. The quarrel is only with the Hobbesian solution. Given man's nature as a rational animal, is the proposed solution to the problem of insecurity an improvement? Can the institution of a state reduce aggressive behavior and promote peaceful cooperation, and thus provide for better private security and protection? The difficulties with Hobbes's argument are obvious. For one, regardless of how bad men are, S—whether king, dictator, or elected president—is still one of them. Man's nature is not transformed upon becoming S. Yet how can there be better protection for A and B, if S must tax them in order to provide it? Is there not a contradiction within the very construction of S as an expropriating property protector? In fact, is this not exactly what is also—and more appropriately—referred to as a *protection racket*? To besure, S will make peace between A and B but only so that he himself in turn can rob both of them more profitably. Surely S is better protected, but the more he is protected, the less A and B are protected from attacks by S. Collective security, it would seem, is not better than private security. Rather, it is the private security of the state, S, achieved through the expropriation, i.e., the economic disarmament, of its subjects. Further, statists from Thomas Hobbes to James Buchanan have argued that a protective state S would come about as the result of some sort of "constitutional" contract.[1] Yet, who in his right mind would agree to a contract that allowed one's protector to determine unilaterally—and irrevocably—the sum that the protected must pay for his protection; and the fact is, no one ever has![2]

Let me interrupt my discussion here, and return to the reconstruction of the Hobbesian myth. Once it is assumed that in order to institute peaceful cooperation between A and B it is necessary to have a state S, a two-fold conclusion follows. If more than one state exists, S1, S2, S3, then, just as there can presumably be no peace among A and B without S, so there can be no peace between the states S1, S2, and S3 as long as they remain in a state of nature (i.e., a state of anarchy) with regard to each other. Consequently, in order to achieve *universal* peace, political centralization, unification, and ultimately the establishment of a single world government are necessary.

Commenting on this argument, it is first useful to indicate what can be taken as non-controversial. To begin with, the argument

---

[1] James M. Buchanan and Gordon Tullock, *The Calculus of Consent* (Ann Arbor: University of Michigan Press, 1962); James M. Buchanan, *The Limits of Liberty* (Chicago: University of Chicago Press, 1975); for a critique see Murray N. Rothbard, "Buchanan and Tullock's *Calculus of Consent*," in idem, *The Logic of Action*, vol. 2, *Applications and Criticism from the Austrian School* (Cheltenham, U.K.: Edward Elgar, 1995); idem, "The Myth of Neutral Taxation," in ibid.; Hans-Hermann Hoppe, *The Economics and Ethics of Private Property* (Boston: Kluwer, 1993), chap. 1.

[2] See on this particular point, Lysander Spooner, *No Treason: The Constitution of No Authority* (Larkspur, Colo.: Pine Tree Press, 1996).

is correct, as far as it goes. If the premise is correct, then the consequence spelled out follows. The empirical assumptions involved in the Hobbesian account appear at first glance to be borne out by the facts, as well. It is true that states are constantly at war with each other, and a historical tendency toward political centralization and global rule does indeed appear to be occurring. Quarrels arise only with the explanation of this fact and tendency, and the classification of a single unified world state as an improvement in the provision of private security and protection. First, there appears to be an empirical anomaly for which the Hobbesian argument cannot account. The reason for the warring among different states S1, S2, and S3, according to Hobbes, is that they are in a state of anarchy *vis-à-vis* each other. However, before the arrival of a single world state not only are S1, S2, and S3 in a state of anarchy relative to each other but in fact every subject of one state is in a state of anarchy *vis-à-vis* every subject of any other state. Accordingly, there should exist just as much war and aggression between the private citizens of various states as between different states. Empirically, however, this is not so. The private dealings between foreigners appear to be significantly less war-like than the dealings between different governments. Nor does this seem to be surprising. After all, a state agent S, in contrast to every one of its subjects, can rely on domestic taxation in the conduct of his foreign affairs. Given his natural human aggressiveness, however pronounced it may initially be, is it not obvious that S will be more brazen and aggressive in his conduct toward foreigners if he can externalize the cost of such behavior onto others? Surely, I am willing to take greater risks and engage in more provocation and aggression if I can make others pay for it. And surely there is a tendency of one state—one protection racket—to want to expand its territorial protection monopoly at the expense of other states and thus bring about, as the ultimate result of interstate competition, world government.[3] But how is this an improvement in the provision of private security and protection? The opposite seems to be the case. The world state is the winner of all wars and the last surviving protection racket. Doesn't this make it particularly dangerous? And will not the physical power of any single world government be overwhelming as compared to that of any one of its individual subjects?

---

[3] See Hans-Hermann Hoppe, "The Trouble With Classical Liberalism," *Rothbard-Rockwell Report* 9, no. 4 (1998).

2. The Empirical Evidence

LET ME PAUSE HERE IN MY ABSTRACT THEORETICAL CONSIDERations to take a brief look at the empirical evidence bearing on the issue at hand. As noted at the outset, the myth of collective security is as widespread as it is consequential. I am not aware of any survey on this matter, but I would venture to predict that the Hobbesian myth is accepted more or less unquestioningly by well over 90 percent of the adult population. However, to believe something does not make it true. Rather, if what one believes is false, one's actions will lead to failure. What about the evidence? Does it support Hobbes and his followers, or does it confirm the opposite anarchist fears and contentions?

The U.S. was explicitly founded as a protective state à la Hobbes. Let me quote to this effect from Jefferson's *Declaration of Independence*:

> We hold these truths to be self-evident: that all men are created equal; that they are endowed by their creator with inalienable rights; that among these are life, liberty, and the pursuit of happiness: that to secure these rights, governments are instituted among men, deriving their just powers from the consent of the governed.

Here we have it: The U.S. government was instituted to fulfill one and only one task: the protection of life and property. Thus, it should provide the perfect example for judging the validity of the Hobbesian claim as to the status of states as protectors. After more than two centuries of protective statism, what is the status of our protection and peaceful human cooperation? Was the American experiment in protective statism a success?

According to the pronouncements of our state rulers and their intellectual bodyguards (of whom there are more than ever before), we are better protected and more secure than ever. We are supposedly protected from global warming and cooling, from the extinction of animals and plants, from the abuses of husbands and wives, parents and employers, from poverty, disease, disaster, ignorance, prejudice, racism, sexism, homophobia, and countless other public enemies and dangers. In fact, however, matters are strikingly different. In order to provide us with all this protection, the state managers expropriate more than 40 percent of the incomes of private producers year in and year out. Government debt and liabilities have increased without interruption, thus increasing the need for future expropriations. Owing to the substitution of government paper money for gold, financial insecurity has increased sharply, and we are continually robbed through currency depreciation. Every detail of private life, property, trade, and contract is regulated by ever higher mountains of laws (legislation), thereby creating permanent legal uncertainty and moral hazard. In particular, we have been gradually stripped of the right to exclusion implied in the very concept of private property. As sellers we cannot sell to and as buyers we cannot buy from whomever we wish. And as members of associations we are not permitted to enter into whatever restrictive covenant we believe to be mutually beneficial. As Americans, we must accept immigrants we do not want as our neighbors. As teachers, we cannot get rid of lousy or ill-behaved students. As employers, we are stuck with incompetent or destructive employees. As landlords, we are forced to cope with bad tenants. As bankers and insurers, we are not allowed to avoid bad risks. As restaurant or bar owners, we must accommodate unwelcome customers. And as members of private associations, we are compelled to accept individuals and actions in violation of our own rules and restrictions. In short, the more the state has increased its expenditures on social security and public safety, the more our private property rights have been eroded, the more our property has been expropriated, confiscated, destroyed, or depreciated, and the more we have been deprived of the very foundation of all protection: economic independence, financial strength, and personal wealth.[4] The path of every president and practically every member of Congress is littered with hundreds of thousands if not millions of nameless victims of personal economic ruin, financial bankruptcy, impoverishment, despair, hardship, and frustration.

The picture appears even bleaker when we consider foreign affairs. Never during its entire history has the continental U.S. been territorially attacked by any foreign army. (Pearl Harbor was the result of a preceding U.S. provocation.) Yet the U.S. has the distinction of having possessed a government that declared war against a large part of its own population and engaged in the wanton murder of hundreds of thousands of its own citizens. Moreover, while the relations between American citizens and foreigners do not appear to be unusually contentious, almost from its very beginnings the U.S. government pursued relentless aggressive expansionism. Beginning with the Spanish-American War, culminating in

---

[4] See Hans-Hermann Hoppe, "Where The Right Goes Wrong," *Rothbard-Rockwell Report* 8, no. 4 (1997).

World War I and World War II, and continuing to the present, the U.S. government has become entangled in hundreds of foreign conflicts and risen to the rank of the world's dominant imperialist power. Thus, nearly every president since the turn of this century also has been responsible for the murder, killing, or starvation of countless innocent foreigners all over the world. In short, while we have become more helpless, impoverished, threatened, and insecure, the U.S. government has become ever more brazen and aggressive. In the name of national security, it defends us, equipped with enormous stockpiles of weapons of aggression and mass destruction, by bullying ever new "Hitlers," big or small, and all suspected Hitlerite sympathizers anywhere and everywhere outside of the territory of the U.S.[5]

The empirical evidence thus seems clear. The belief in a protective state appears to be a patent error, and the American experiment in protective statism a complete failure. The U.S. government does not protect us. To the contrary, there exists no greater danger to our life, property, and prosperity than the U.S. government, and the U.S. president in particular is the world's single most threatening and armed danger, capable of ruining everyone who opposes him and destroying the entire globe.

---

[5] See John Denson, ed., *The Costs of War* (New Brunswick, N.J.: Transaction Publishers, 1997).

3. How to Think About the Statist Response

STATISTS REACT MUCH LIKE SOCIALISTS WHEN FACED WITH THE dismal economic performance of the Soviet Union and its satellites. They do not necessarily deny the disappointing facts, but they try to argue them away by claiming that these facts are the result of a systematic discrepancy (deviancy) between "real" and "ideal" or "true" statism, respectively socialism. To this day, socialists claim that "true" socialism has not been refuted by the empirical evidence, and everything would have turned out well and unparalleled prosperity would have resulted, if only Trotsky's, or Bucharin's, or better still their very own brand of socialism, rather than Stalin's, had been implemented. Similarly, statists interpret all seemingly contradictory evidence as only accidental. If only some other president had come to power at this or that turn in history, or if only this or that constitutional change or amendment had been adopted, everything would have turned out beautifully, and unparalleled security and peace would have resulted. Indeed, this may still happen in the future, if their own policies are employed.

We have learned from Ludwig von Mises how to respond to the socialists' evasion (immunization) strategy.[6] As long as

---

[6] Ludwig von Mises, *Socialism* (Indianapolis: Liberty Classics, 1981); Hans-Hermann Hoppe, *A Theory of Socialism and Capitalism* (Boston:

the defining characteristic—the essence—of socialism, i.e., the absence of the private ownership of the factors of production, remains in place, no reform will be of any help. The idea of a socialist economy is a *contradictio in adjecto*, and the claim that socialism represents a higher, more efficient mode of social production is absurd. In order to reach one's own ends efficiently and without waste within the framework of an exchange economy based on division of labor, it is necessary that one engage in monetary calculation(cost-accounting). Everywhere outside the system of a primitive self-sufficient single household economy, monetary calculation is the sole tool of rational and efficient action. Only by being able to compare inputs and outputs arithmetically in terms of a common medium of exchange (money) can a person determine whether his actions are successful or not. In distinct contrast, socialism means to have no economy, no economizing, at all, because under these conditions monetary calculation and cost-accounting is impossible by definition. If no private property in the factors of production exists, then no prices for any production factor exist; hence, it is impossible to determine whether or not they are employed economically. Accordingly, socialism is not a higher mode of production but rather economic chaos and regression to primitivism.

How to respond to the statists' evasion strategy has been explained by Murray N. Rothbard.[7] But Rothbard's lesson, while equally simple and clear and with even more momentous implications, has remained to this day far less known and appreciated. So long as the defining characteristic—the essence—of a state remains in place, he explained, no reform,

---

Kluwer, 1989), chap. 6.

[7] Murray N. Rothbard, *The Ethics of Liberty* (New York: New York University Press, 1998), esp. chaps. 22 and 23.

whether on the level of personnel or of the constitution, will be to any avail. *Given* the principle of government—judicial monopoly and the power to tax—any notion of limiting its power and safeguarding individual life and property is illusory. Under monopolistic auspices the price of justice and protection must rise and its quality must fall. A tax-funded protection agency is a contradiction in terms and will lead to ever more taxes and less protection. Even if a government limited its activities exclusively to the protection of pre-existing property rights (as every protective state is supposed to do), the further question of *how much* security to provide would arise. Motivated (like everyone else) by self-interest and the disutility of labor, but with the unique power to tax, a government's answer will invariably be the same: to *maximize expenditures* on protection—and almost all of a nation's wealth can conceivably be consumed by the cost of protection—and at the same time to *minimize* the *production* of protection. Furthermore, a judicial monopoly must lead to a deterioration in the quality of justice and protection. If one can only appeal to government for justice and protection, justice and protection will be perverted in favor of government, constitutions, and supreme courts notwithstanding. After all, constitutions and supreme courts are *state* constitutions and courts, and whatever limitations to government action they might contain is determined by agents of the very institution under consideration. Accordingly, the definition of property and protection will continually be altered and the range of jurisdiction expanded to the government's advantage.

Hence, Rothbard pointed out, it follows that just as socialism cannot be reformed but must be abolished in order to achieve prosperity, so can the institution of a state not be reformed but must be abolished in order to achieve justice and protection. "Defense in the free society (including such defense services to person and property as police protection and judicial findings)," Rothbard concluded, "would therefore have to be supplied by people or firms who (a) gained their revenue voluntarily rather than by coercion and (b) did not—as the State does—arrogate to themselves a compulsory monopoly of police or judicial protection... defense firms would have to be as freely competitive and as noncoercive against noninvaders as are all other suppliers of goods and services on the free market. Defense services, like all other services, would be marketable and marketable only."[8] That is, every private property owner would be able to partake of the advantages of the division of labor and seek better protection of his property than that afforded through self-defense by cooperation with other owners and their property. Anyone could buy from, sell to, or otherwise contract with anyone else concerning protective and judicial services, and one could at any time unilaterally discontinue any such cooperation with others and fall back on self-reliant defense, or change one's protective affiliations.

---

[8] Murray N. Rothbard, *Power and Market* (Kansas City: Sheed Andrews and McMeel, 1977), p. 2.

4. The Case for Private Security

HAVING RECONSTRUCTED THE MYTH OF COLLECTIVE SECURITY—the myth of the state—and criticized it on theoretical and empirical grounds, I now must take on the task of constructing the positive case for private security and protection. In order to dispel the myth of collective security, it is not just sufficient to grasp the *error* involved in the idea of a protective state. It is just as important, if not more so, to gain a clear understanding of how the non-statist security alternative would effectively work. Rothbard, building on the pathbreaking analysis of the French-Belgian economist Gustave de Molinari,[9] has given us a sketch of the workings of a free-market system of protection and defense.[10] As well, we owe Morris and Linda Tannehill for their brilliant insights and analyses in this regard.[11] Following their lead, I will proceed deeper in my analysis and provide a more *comprehensive* view of the alternative–non-statist-system

---

[9] Gustave de Molinari, *The Production of Security* (New York: Center for Libertarian Studies, 1977).

[10] Murray N. Rothbard, *Power and Market*, chap. 1; idem, *For A New Liberty* (New York: Collier, 1978), chaps. 12 and 14.

[11] Morris and Linda Tannehill, *The Market for Liberty* (New York: Laissez Faire Books, 1984), esp. part 2.

of security production and its ability to handle attacks, not just by individuals or gangs but in particular also by *states*.

There exists widespread agreement—among liberal-libertarians such as Molinari, Rothbard, and the Tannehills as well as most other commentators on the matter—that defense is a form of insurance, and defense expenditures represent a sort of insurance premium (price). Accordingly, as Rothbard and the Tannehills in particular would emphasize, within the framework of a complex modern economy based on a worldwide division of labor the most likely candidates for offering protection and defense services are insurance agencies. The better the protection of insured property, the lower are the damage claims and hence an insurer's costs. Thus, to provide efficient protection appears to be in every insurer's own financial interest; and in fact even now, although restricted and hampered by the state, insurance agencies provide wide-ranging services of protection and indemnification (compensation) to injured private parties. Insurance companies fulfill a second essential requirement. Obviously, anyone offering protection services must appear able to deliver on his promises in order to find clients. That is, he must possess the economic means—the manpower as well as the physical resources—necessary to accomplish the task of dealing with the dangers, actual or imagined, of the real world. On this count insurance agencies appear to be perfect candidates, too. They operate on a nationwide and even international scale, and they own large property holdings dispersed over wide territories and beyond single state boundaries. Accordingly, they have a manifest self-interest in effective protection, and are big and economically powerful. Furthermore, all insurance companies are connected through a network of contractual agreements of mutual assistance and arbitration as well as a system of international reinsurance agencies, representing a combined economic power which dwarfs that of most if not all existing governments.

I want to further analyze and systematically clarify this suggestion: that protection and defense are insurance and can be provided by insurance agencies. To reach this goal, two issues must be addressed. First, it is not possible to insure oneself against every risk of life. I cannot insure myself against committing suicide, for instance, or against burning down my own house, or becoming unemployed, or not feeling like getting out of bed in the morning, or not suffering entrepreneurial losses, because in each case I have full or partial control over the likelihood of the respective outcome. Risks such as these must be assumed individually. No one except myself can possibly deal with them. Hence, the first question will have to be what makes protection and defense an insurable rather than an uninsurable risk? After all, as we have just seen, this is not self-evident. In fact, doesn't everyone have considerable control over the likelihood of an attack on and invasion of his person and property? Do I not deliberately bring about an attack by assaulting or provoking someone else, for instance, and is not protection then an uninsurable risk, like suicide or unemployment, for which each person must assume sole responsibility?

The answer is a qualified yes and no. Yes, insofar as no one can possibly offer *un*conditional protection, i.e., insurance against any invasion whatsoever. That is, unconditional protection can only be provided, if at all, by each individual on his own and for himself. But the answer is no, *insofar* as conditional protection is concerned. Only attacks and invasions that are provoked by the victim cannot be insured. However, unprovoked and thus accidental attacks can be insured against.[12] That is, protection becomes an insurable good only

---

[12] On the "logic" of insurance see Ludwig von Mises, *Human Action* (Chicago: Regnery, 1966), chap. 6; Murray N. Rothbard, *Man, Economy, and State* (Auburn, Ala.: Ludwig von Mises Institute, 1993), pp.

if and insofar as an insurance agent contractually restricts the actions of the insured so as to exclude every possible provocation on their part. Various insurance companies may differ with respect to the specific definition of provocation, but there can be no difference between insurers with regard to the principle that each must systematically exclude (prohibit) all provocative and aggressive action among its own clients.

As elementary as this first insight into the essentially defensive—non-aggressive and nonprovocative—nature of protection-insurance may seem, it is of fundamental importance. For one, it implies that any known aggressor and provocateur would be unable to find an insurer, and hence, would be economically isolated, weak, and vulnerable. On the other hand, it implies that anyone wanting more protection than that afforded by self-reliant self-defense could do so only if and insofar as he submitted himself to specified norms of non-aggressive, civilized conduct. Furthermore, the greater the number of insured people—and in a modern exchange economy most people want more than just self-defense for their protection—the greater would be the economic pressure on the remaining uninsured to adopt the same or similar standards of non-aggressive social conduct. Moreover, as the result of competition between insurers for voluntarily paying clients, a tendency toward falling prices per insured property values would come about. At the same time, a tendency toward the standardization and unification of property and contract law would be set in motion. Protection contracts with standardized property and product

---

498ff.; Hans-Hermann Hoppe, "On Certainty and Uncertainty, Or: How Rational Can Our Expectations Be?" *Review of Austrian Economics* 10, no. 1 (1997); also Richard von Mises, *Probability, Statistics, and Truth* (New York: Dover, 1957); Frank H. Knight, *Risk, Uncertainty, and Profit* (Chicago: University of Chicago Press, 1971).

descriptions would come into existence; and out of the steady cooperation between different insurers in mutual arbitration proceedings, a tendency toward the standardization and unification of the rules of procedure, evidence, and conflict resolution (including compensation, restitution, punishment, and retribution), and steadily increasing legal certainty would result. Everyone, by virtue of buying protection insurance, would be tied into a global competitive enterprise of striving to minimize aggression (and thus maximize defensive protection), and every single conflict and damage claim, regardless of where and by or against whom, would fall into the jurisdiction of exactly one or more enumerable and specific insurance agencies and their mutually defined arbitration procedures.

5. More on Aggression Insurance

NOW A SECOND QUESTION MUST BE ADDRESSED. EVEN IF THE status of defensive protection as an insurable good is granted, distinctly different forms of insurance exist. Let us consider just two characteristic examples: insurance against natural disasters, such as earthquakes, floods, and hurricanes and insurance against industrial accidents or disasters, such as malfunctions, explosions, or defective products. The former can serve as an example of group or mutual insurance. Some territories are more prone to natural disasters than others; as a result the demand for and price of insurance will be higher in some areas than others. However, every location *within* certain territorial borders is regarded by the insurer as homogeneous with respect to the risk concerned. The insurer presumably knows the frequency and extent of the event in question for the region as a whole, but he knows nothing about the particular risk of any specific location within the territory. In this case, every insured person will pay the same premium per insured value, and the premiums collected in one time period are presumably sufficient to cover all damage claims during the same time period (otherwise the insurance industry will have losses). Thus, the particular individual risks are pooled and insured mutually.

In contrast, industrial insurance can serve as an example of individual insurance. Unlike natural disasters, the insured risk is the outcome of human action, i.e., of production efforts. Every production process is under the control of an individual producer. No producer *intends* failure or disaster, and as we have seen only accidental—non-intended—disasters are insurable. Yet even if largely controlled and generally successful, every producer and production technology is subject to occasional mishaps and accidents beyond his control—a margin of error. However, as the outcome, even if unintended, of individual production efforts and production techniques, this risk of industrial accidents is essentially different from one producer and production process to another. Accordingly, the risk of different producers and production technologies cannot be pooled, and every producer must be insured individually. In this case, the insurer presumably will have to know the frequency of the questionable event over time, but he knows nothing of the likelihood of the event at any specific point in time, except that at all times the same producer and production technology is in operation. There is no presumption that the premiums collected during any given period will be sufficient to cover all damage claims arising during that period. Rather, the profit-making presumption is that all premiums collected over many time periods will be sufficient in order to cover all claims during the same multi-period time span. Consequently, in this case an insurer must hold capital reserves in order to fulfill its contractual obligation, and in calculating his premiums he must take the present value of these reserves into account.

The second question is, then, what kind of insurance can protect against aggression and invasion by other actors? Can it be provided as group insurance, as for natural disasters, or will it have to be offered in the form of individual insurance, as in the case of industrial accidents?

Let me note at the outset that both forms of insurance represent only the two possible extremes of a continuum, and that the position of any particular risk on this continuum is not definitively fixed. Owing to scientific and technological advances in meteorology, geology, or engineering, for instance, risks that were formerly regarded as homogeneous (allowing for mutual insurance) can become more and more de-homogenized. Noteworthy is this tendency in the field of medical and health insurance. With the advances of genetics and genetic engineering—genetic fingerprinting—medical and health risks previously regarded as homogeneous (unspecific) with respect to large numbers of people have become increasingly more specific and heterogeneous.

With this in mind, can anything specific be said about protection insurance in particular? I would think so. After all, while all insurance requires that the risk be accidental from the standpoint of the insurer and the insured, the accident of an aggressive invasion is distinctly different from that of natural or industrial disasters. Whereas natural disasters and industrial accidents are the outcome of natural forces and the operation of laws of nature, aggression is the outcome of human actions; and whereas nature is blind and does not discriminate between individuals, whether at the same point in time or over time, an aggressor can discriminate and deliberately target specific victims and choose the timing of his attack.

6. Political Borders and Insurance

LET ME FIRST CONTRAST DEFENSE-PROTECTION INSURANCE WITH that against natural disasters. Frequently an analogy between the two is drawn, and it is instructive to examine if or to what extent it holds. The analogy is that just as every individual within certain geographical regions is threatened by the same risk of earthquakes, floods, or hurricanes, so does every inhabitant within the territory of the U.S. or Germany, for instance, face the same risk of being victimized by a foreign attack. Some superficial similarity—to which I shall come shortly—notwithstanding, it is easy to recognize two fundamental shortcomings in the analogy. For one, the borders of earthquake, flood, or hurricane regions are established and drawn according to objective physical criteria and hence can be referred to as natural. In distinct contrast, political boundaries are artificial boundaries. The borders of the U.S. changed throughout the entire 19th century, and Germany did not exist as such until 1871, but was composed of nearly 50 separate countries. Surely, no one would want to claim that this redrawing of the U.S. or German borders was the outcome of the discovery that the security risk of every American or German within the greater U.S. or Germany was, contrary to the previously held opposite belief, homogeneous (identical).

There is a second obvious shortcoming. Nature—earthquakes, floods, hurricanes—is blind in its destruction. It does not discriminate between more and less valuable locations and objects, but attacks indiscriminately. In distinct contrast, an aggressor-invader can and does discriminate. He does not attack or invade worthless locations and things, like the Sahara Desert, but targets locations and things that are valuable. Other things being equal, the more valuable a location and an object, the more likely it will be the target of an invasion.

This raises the crucial next question. If political borders are arbitrary and attacks are in any case never indiscriminate but directed specifically toward valuable places and things, are there any non-arbitrary borders separating different security-risk (attack) zones? The answer is yes. Such non-arbitrary borders are those of private property. Private property is the result of the appropriation and/or production of particular physical objects or effects by specific individuals at specific locations. Every appropriator-producer (owner) demonstrates with his actions that he regards the appropriated and produced things as valuable (goods), otherwise he would not have appropriated or produced them. The borders of everyone's property are objective and intersubjectively ascertainable. They are simply determined by the extension and dimension of the things appropriated and/or produced by any one particular individual. And the borders of all valuable places and things are coextensive with the borders of all property. At any given point in time, every valuable place and thing is owned by someone; only worthless places and things are owned by no one.

Surrounded by other men, every appropriator and producer can also become the object of an attack or invasion. Every property—in contrast to things (matter)—is necessarily valuable; hence, every property owner becomes a possible target of other men's aggressive desires. Consequently, every owner's choice of the location and form of his property will, among countless other considerations, also be influenced by security concerns. Other things being equal, everyone will prefer safer locations and forms of property to locations and forms which are less safe. Yet, regardless of where an owner and his property are located and whatever the property's physical form, every owner, by virtue of not abandoning his property even in view of potential aggression, demonstrates his personal willingness to protect and defend these possessions.

However, if the borders of private property are the only non-arbitrary borders standing in systematic relation to the risk of aggression, then it follows that as many different security zones as there are separately owned property holdings exist, and that these zones are no larger than the extension of these holdings. That is, even more so than in the case of industrial accidents, the insurance of property against aggression would seem to be an example of individual rather than group (mutual) protection.

Whereas the accident-risk of an individual production process is typically independent of its location—such that if the process were replicated by the same producer at different locations his margin of error would remain the same—the risk of aggression against private property—the production plant—is different from one location to another. By its very nature, as privately appropriated and produced goods, property is always separate and distinct. Every property is located at a different place and under the control of a different individual, and each location faces a unique security risk. It can make a difference for my security, for instance, if I reside in the countryside or the city, on a hill or in a valley, or near or far from a river, ocean, harbor, railroad or street. In fact, even contiguous locations do not face the same risk. It can make a difference, for instance, if I reside higher or lower on the mountain than my neighbor, upstream or downstream, closer to or more distant from the ocean, or simply north, south, west, or east of him. Moreover, every property, wherever it is located, can be shaped and transformed by its owner so as to increase its safety and reduce the likelihood of an aggression. I may acquire a gun or safe-deposit box, for instance, or I may be able to shoot down an attacking plane from my backyard or own a laser gun that can kill an aggressor thousands of miles away. Thus, no location and no property are like any other. Every owner will have to be insured individually, and to do so every aggression-insurer must hold sufficient capital reserves.

7. The Democratic State and Total War

THE ANALOGY TYPICALLY DRAWN BETWEEN INSURANCE AGAINST natural disasters and external aggression is fundamentally flawed. As aggression is never indiscriminate but selective and targeted, so is defense. Everyone has different locations and things to defend, and no one's security risk is the same as anyone else's. And yet the analogy also contains a kernel of truth. However, any similarity between natural disasters and external aggression is due *not* to the nature of aggression and defense but to the rather specific nature of *state*-aggression and defense (interstate warfare). As explained above, a state is an agency that exercises a compulsory territorial monopoly of protection and the power to tax, and any such agency will be comparatively more aggressive because it can externalize the costs of such behavior onto its subjects. However, the existence of a state does not just increase the frequency of aggression; it changes its entire character. The existence of states, and especially of democratic states, implies that aggression and defense—war—will tend to be transformed into total, undiscriminating, war.[13]

---

[13] On the relationship between state and war, and on the historical transformation from limited (monarchical) to total (democratic) war, see Ekkehard Krippendorff, *Staat and Krieg* (Frankfurt/M.: Suhrkamp,

Consider for a moment a completely stateless world. Most property owners would be individually insured by large, often multinational insurance companies endowed with huge capital reserves. Most if not all aggressors, being bad risks, would be left without any insurance whatever. In this situation, every aggressor or group of aggressors would want to limit their targets, preferably to uninsured property, and avoid all "collateral damage," as they would otherwise find themselves confronted with one or many economically powerful professional defense agencies. Likewise, all defensive violence would be highly selective and targeted. All aggressors would be specific individuals or groups, located at specific places and equipped with specific resources. In response to attacks on their clients, insurance agencies would specifically target these locations and resources for retaliation, and they would want to avoid any collateral damage as they would otherwise become entangled with and liable to other insurers.

All of this fundamentally changes in a statist world with interstate warfare. For one, if a state, the U.S., attacks another, for instance Iraq, this is not just an attack by a limited number of people, equipped with limited resources and located at a clearly identifiable place. Rather, it is an attack by all Americans and with all of their resources. Every American

---

1985); Charles Tilly, "War Making and State Making as Organized Crime," in *Bringing the State Back In*, Peter B. Evans, Dietrich Rueschemeyer, Theda Skocpol, eds. (Cambridge: Cambridge University Press, 1985); John F.C. Fuller, *The Conduct of War* (New York: Da Capo Press, 1992); Michael Howard, *War in European History* (New York: Oxford University Press, 1976); Hans-Hermann Hoppe, "Time Preference, Government, and the Process of De-Civilization," in *The Costs of War*, John V. Denson, ed. (New Brunswick, N.J.: Transaction Publishers, 1997); Erik von Kuehnelt-Leddihn, *Leftism Revisited* (Washington, D.C.: Regnery, 1990).

supposedly pays taxes to the U.S. government and is thus *de facto*, whether he wishes to be or not, implicated in every government aggression. Hence, while it is obviously false to claim that every American faces an equal risk of being attacked by Iraq, (low or nonexistent as such a risk is, it is certainly higher in New York City than in Wichita, Kansas, for instance) every American is rendered equal with respect to his own active, if not always voluntary, participation in each of his government's aggressions.

Second, just as the attacker is a state, so is the attacked, Iraq. As its U.S. counterpart, the Iraqi government has the power to tax its population or draft it into its armed forces. As taxpayer or draftee, every Iraqi is implicated in his government's defense just as every American is drawn into the U.S. government's attack. Thus, the war becomes a war of all Americans against all Iraqis, i.e., total war. The strategy of both the attacker and the defender state will be changed accordingly. While the attacker still must be selective regarding the targets of his attack, if for no other reason than that even taxing agencies (states) are ultimately constrained by scarcity, the aggressor has little or no incentive to avoid or minimize collateral damage. To the contrary, since the entire population and national wealth is involved in the defensive effort, collateral damage, whether of lives or property, is even desirable. No clear distinction between combatants and non-combatants exists. Everyone is an enemy, and all property provides support for the attacked government. Hence, everyone and everything becomes fair game. Likewise, the defender state will be little concerned about collateral damage resulting from its own retaliation against the attacker. Every citizen of the attacker state and all of their property is a foe and enemy property and thus becomes a possible target of retaliation. Moreover, every state, in accordance with this character of interstate war, will develop and employ more weapons of mass destruction, such as atomic bombs, rather than long-range precision weapons, such as my imaginary laser gun.

Thus, the similarity between war and natural catastrophes—their seemingly indiscriminate destruction and devastation—is exclusively a feature of a statist world.

8. Insurance and Incentives

THIS BRINGS ON THE LAST PROBLEM. WE HAVE SEEN THAT JUST AS all property is private, all defense must be insured individually by capitalized insurance agencies, very much like industrial accident insurance. Yet, we have also seen that both forms of insurance differ in one fundamental respect. In the case of defense insurance, the location of the insured property matters. The premium per insured value will be different at different locations. Furthermore, aggressors can move around, their arsenal of weapons may change, and their entire character of aggression can alter with the presence of states. Thus, even given an initial property location, the price per insured value can alter with changes in the social environment or surroundings of this location. How would a system of competitive insurance agencies respond to this challenge? In particular, how would it deal with the existence of states and state aggression?

In answering these questions it is essential to recall some elementary economic insights. Other things being equal, private property owners generally, and business owners in particular, prefer locations with low protection costs (insurance premiums) and rising property values to those with high protection costs and falling property values. Consequently, there is a tendency toward the migration of people and goods from high risk and falling property value areas into low risk and increasing property value areas. Furthermore, protection costs and property values are directly related. Other things being equal, higher protection costs (greater attack risks) imply lower or falling property values, and lower protection costs imply higher or increasing property values. These laws and tendencies shape the operation of a competitive system of insurance-protection agencies.

First, whereas a tax-funded monopolist will manifest a tendency to raise the cost and price of protection, private profit-loss insurance agencies strive to reduce the cost of protection and thus bring about falling prices. At the same time insurance agencies are more interested than anyone else in rising property values, because this implies not only that their own property holdings appreciate but in particular that there will also be more of other people's property for them to insure. In contrast, if the risk of aggression increases and property values fall, there is less value to be insured while the cost of protection and price of insurance rises, implying poor business conditions for an insurer. Consequently, insurance companies would be under permanent economic pressure to promote the former favorable and avert the latter unfavorable condition.

This incentive structure has a fundamental impact on the operation of insurers. For one, as for the seemingly easier case of the protection against common crime and criminals, a system of competitive insurers would lead to a dramatic change in current crime policy. To recognize the extent of this change, it is instructive to look first at the present and thus familiar statist crime policy. While it is in the interest of state agents to combat common private crime (if only so that there is more property left for them to tax), as tax-funded agents they have little or no interest in being particularly effective at the task of preventing it, or else, if it has occurred, at compensating its victims and apprehending and punishing the offenders.

Moreover, under democratic conditions, insult will be added to injury. For if everyone—aggressors as well as non-aggressors and residents of high crime locations as well as those of low crime locations—can vote and be elected to government office, a systematic redistribution of property rights from non-aggressors to aggressors and the residents of low crime areas to those of high crime areas comes into effect and crime will actually be promoted. Accordingly, crime, and consequently the demand for private security services of all kinds are currently at an all-time high. Even more scandalously, instead of compensating the victims of crimes it did not prevent (as it should have), the government forces victims to pay again as taxpayers for the cost of the apprehension, imprisonment, rehabilitation, and/or entertainment of their aggressors. And rather than requiring higher protection prices in high crime locations and lower ones in low crime locations, as insurers would, the government does the exact opposite. It taxes more in low crime and high property value areas than in high crime and low property value ones, or it even subsidizes the residents of the latter locations—the slums—at the expense of those of the former and thus erodes the social conditions unfavorable to crime while promoting those favorable to it.[14]

---

[14] On crime and punishment, past and present, see Terry Anderson and P.J. Hill, "The American Experiment in Anarcho-Capitalism: The Not So Wild, Wild West," *Journal of Libertarian Studies* 3, no. 1 (1979); Bruce L. Benson, "Guns for Protection, and Other Private Sector Responses to the Government's Failure to Control Crime," *Journal of Libertarian Studies* 8, no. 1 (1986); Roger D. McGrath, *Gunfighters, Highwaymen, and Vigilantes: Violence on the Frontier* (Berkeley: University of California Press, 1984); James Q. Wilson and Richard J. Herrnstien, *Crime and Human Nature* (New York: Simon and Schuster, 1985); Edward C. Banfield, *The Unheavenly City Revisited* (Boston: Little, Brown, 1974).

The operation of competitive insurers would be in striking contrast. For one, if an insurer could not prevent a crime, it would have to indemnify the victim. Thus, above all insurers would want to be effective in crime prevention. And if they still could not prevent it, they would want to be efficient in the detection, apprehension, and punishment of criminal offenders, because in finding and arresting an offender, the insurer could force the criminal—rather than the victim and its insurer—to pay for the damages and cost of indemnification.

More specifically, just as insurance companies currently maintain and continually update a detailed local inventory of property values so they would then maintain and continually update a detailed local inventory of crimes and criminals. Other things being equal, the risk of aggression against any private property location increases with the proximity and the number and resources of potential aggressors. Thus, insurers would be interested in gathering information on actual crimes and known criminals and their locations, and it would be in their mutual interest of minimizing property damage to share this information with each other (just as banks now share information on bad credit risks with each other). Furthermore, insurers would also be particularly interested in gathering information on potential (not yet committed and known) crimes and aggressors, and this would lead to a fundamental overhaul of and improvement in current—statist—crime statistics. In order to predict the future incidence of crime and thus calculate its current price (premium), insurers would correlate the frequency, description, and character of crimes and criminals with the social surroundings in which they occur and operate, and develop and under competitive pressure continually refine an elaborate system of demographic and sociological crime indicators.[15] That is, every neighborhood would be described, and its risk assessed, in terms and in light of a multitude of crime indicators, such as the composition of sexes, age groups, races, nationalities, ethnicities, religions, languages, professions, and incomes.

Consequently, and in distinct contrast to the present situation, all interlocal, regional, racial, national, ethnic, religious, and linguistic income, and wealth redistribution would disappear, and a constant source of social conflict would be removed permanently. Instead, the emerging price (premium) structure would tend to accurately reflect the risk of each location and its particular social surrounding, such that no one would be forced to pay for the insurance risk of anyone but his own and that associated with his particular neighborhood. More importantly, based on its continually updated and refined system of statistics on crime and property values and further motivated by the noted migration tendency from high-risk-low-value (henceforth "bad") to low-risk-high-value (henceforth "good") locations, a system of competitive aggression insurers would promote a tendency toward civilizational progress (rather than decivilization).

Governments—and democratic governments in particular—erode "good" and promote "bad" neighborhoods through their tax and transfer policy. They do so also, and with possibly an even more damaging effect, through their policy of forced integration. This policy has two aspects. On the one hand, for the owners and residents in "good" locations and

---

[15] For an overview of the extent to which official—statist—statistics, in particular on crime, deliberately ignore, misrepresent, or distort the known facts for reason of so-called public policy (political correctness) see J. Philippe Rushton, *Race, Evolution, and Behavior* (New Brunswick, N.J.: Transaction Publishers, 1995); Michael Levin, *Why Race Matters* (Westport, Conn.: Praeger, 1997).

neighborhoods who are faced with an immigration problem, forced integration means that they must accept, without discrimination, every domestic immigrant, as transient or tourist on public roads, as customer, client, resident, or neighbor. They are prohibited by their government from excluding anyone, including anyone they consider an undesirable potential risk, from immigration. On the other hand, for the owners and residents in "bad" locations and neighborhoods, who experience emigration rather than immigration, forced integration means that they are prevented from effective self-protection. Rather than being allowed to rid themselves of crime through the expulsion of known criminals from their neighborhood, they are forced by their government to live in permanent association with their aggressors.[16]

The results of a system of private protection insurers would be in striking contrast to these all too familiar de-civilizing effects and tendencies of statist crime protection. To be sure, insurers would be unable to eliminate the differences between "good" and "bad" neighborhoods. In fact, these differences might even become more pronounced. However, driven by their interest in rising property values and falling protection costs, insurers would promote a tendency to improve by uplifting and cultivating both "good" and "bad" neighborhoods. Thus, in "good" neighborhoods insurers would adopt a policy of selective immigration. Unlike states, they could not and would not want to disregard the discriminating inclinations among the insured toward immigrants. To the contrary, even more so than any one of their clients, insurers would be interested in discrimination: in admitting only those immigrants whose presence adds to a lower crime risk and increased

---

[16] See Hans-Hermann Hoppe, "Free Immigration or Forced Integration," *Chronicles* (July 1995).

property values and in excluding those whose presence leads to a higher risk and lower property values. That is, rather than eliminating discrimination, insurers would rationalize and perfect its practice. Based on their statistics on crime and property values, and in order to reduce the cost of protection and raise property values, insurers would formulate and continually refine various restrictive (exclusionary) rules and procedures relating to immigration and immigrants and thus give quantitative precision—in the form of prices and price differentials—to the value of discrimination (and the cost of non-discrimination) between potential immigrants (as high or low risk and value-productive).

Similarly, in "bad" neighborhoods the interests of the insurers and the insured would coincide. Insurers would not want to suppress the expulsionist inclinations among the insured toward known criminals. They would rationalize such tendencies by offering selective price cuts (contingent on specific clean-up operations). Indeed, in cooperation with one another, insurers would want to expel known criminals not just from their immediate neighborhood, but from civilization altogether, into the wilderness or open frontier of the Amazon jungle, the Sahara, or the polar regions.

9. Insuring Against State Aggression

YET WHAT ABOUT DEFENSE AGAINST A STATE? HOW WOULD insurers protect us from state aggression?

First, it is essential to remember that governments qua compulsory, tax-funded monopolies are inherently wasteful and inefficient in whatever they do. This is also true for weapons technology and production, military intelligence and strategy, especially in our age of high technology. Accordingly, states would not be able to compete within the same territory against voluntarily financed insurance agencies. Moreover, most important and general among the restrictive rules relating to immigration and designed by insurers to lower protection cost and increase property values would be one concerning government agents. States are inherently aggressive and pose a permanent danger to every insurer and insured. Thus, insurers in particular would want to exclude or severely restrict—as a potential security risk—the immigration (territorial entry) of all known government agents, and they would induce the insured, either as a condition of insurance or of a lower premium, to exclude or strictly limit any direct contact with any known government agent, be it as visitor, customer, client, resident, or neighbor. That is, wherever insurance companies operated—in all free territories—state agents would be treated as undesirable outcasts, potentially more dangerous than any common criminal. Accordingly, states and their personnel would be able to operate and reside only in territorial separation from, and on the fringes of, free territories. Furthermore, owing to the comparatively lower economic productivity of statist territories, governments would be continually weakened by the emigration of their most value-productive residents.

Now, what if such a government should decide to attack or invade a free territory? This would be easier said than done! Who and what would one attack? There would be no state opponent. Only private property owners and their private insurance agencies would exist. No one, least of all the insurers, would have presumably engaged in aggression or even provocation. If there were any aggression or provocation against the state at all, this would be the action of a particular person, and in this case the interest of the state and insurance agencies would fully coincide. Both would want to see the attacker punished and held accountable for all damages caused. But without any aggressor-enemy, how could the state justify an attack and even more so any indiscriminate attack? And surely it would have to justify it! For the power of every government, even the most despotic one, rests ultimately on opinion and consent, as la Boétie, Hume, Mises and Rothbard have explained.[17] Kings and presidents can issue an order to attack, of course. But there must be scores of other men willing to execute their order to put it into effect. There must be

---

[17] Etienne de la Boétie, *The Politics of Obedience: The Discourse of Voluntary Servitude* (New York: Free Life Editions, 1975); David Hume, "The First Principles of Government," in idem, *Essays: Moral, Political, and Literary* (Oxford: Oxford University Press, 1971); Ludwig von Mises, *Liberalism: In the Classical Tradition* (San Francisco: Cobden Press, 1985); Murray N. Rothbard, *Egalitarianism As A Revolt Against Nature and Other Essays* (Washington, D.C.: Libertarian Review Press, 1974.).

generals receiving and following the order, soldiers willing to march, kill, and be killed, and domestic producers willing to continue producing to fund the war. If this consensual willingness were absent because the orders of the state rulers were considered illegitimate, even the seemingly most powerful government would be rendered ineffectual and collapse, as the recent examples of the Shah of Iran and the Soviet Union have illustrated. Hence, from the viewpoint of the leaders of the state an attack on free territories would have to be considered extremely risky. No propaganda effort, however elaborate, would make the public believe that its attack were anything but an aggression against innocent victims. In this situation, the rulers of the state would be happy to maintain monopolistic control over their present territory rather than running the risk of losing legitimacy and all of their power in an attempt at territorial expansion.

However, as unlikely as this may be, what would happen if a state still attacked and/or invaded a neighboring free territory? In this case the aggressor would not encounter an unarmed population. Only in statist territories is the civilian population characteristically unarmed. States everywhere aim to disarm their own citizenry so as to be better able to tax and expropriate it. In contrast, insurers in free territories would not want to disarm the insured. Nor could they. For who would want to be protected by someone who required him as a first step to give up his ultimate means of self-defense? To the contrary, insurance agencies would encourage the ownership of weapons among their insured by means of selective price cuts.

Moreover, apart from the opposition of an armed private citizenry, the aggressor state would run into the resistance of not only one but in all likelihood several insurance and reinsurance agencies. In the case of a successful attack and invasion, these insurers would be faced with massive indemnification payments.

Unlike the aggressing state, however, these insurers would be efficient and competitive firms. Other things being equal, the risk of an attack—and hence the price of defense insurance—would be higher in locations adjacent or in close proximity to state territories than in places far away from any state. To justify this higher price, insurers would have to demonstrate defensive readiness *vis-à-vis* any possible state aggression to their clients, in the form of intelligence services, the ownership of suitable weapons and materials, and military personnel and training. In other words, the insurers would be prepared—effectively equipped and trained—for the contingency of a state attack and ready to respond with a two-fold defense strategy. On the one hand, insofar as their operations in free territories are concerned insurers would be ready to expel, capture, or kill every invader while at the same time trying to avoid or minimize all collateral damage. On the other hand, insofar as their operations on state territory are concerned insurers would be prepared to target the aggressor—the state—for retaliation. That is, insurers would be ready to counterattack and kill, whether with long-range precision weapons or assassination commandos, state agents from the top of the government hierarchy of king, president, or prime minister on downward while at the same time seeking to avoid or minimize all collateral damage to the property of innocent civilians (non-state agents), and they would thereby encourage internal resistance against the aggressor government, promote its delegitimization, and possibly incite the liberation and transformation of the state territory into a free country.

10. Regaining Our Right to Self-Defense

I HAVE THUS COME FULL CIRCLE WITH MY ARGUMENT. FIRST, I HAVE shown that the idea of a protective state and state protection of private property is based on a fundamental theoretical error, and that this error has had disastrous consequences: the destruction and insecurity of all private property and perpetual war. Second, I have shown that the correct answer to the question of who is to defend private property owners from aggression is the same as for the production of every other good or service: private property owners, cooperation based on the division of labor, and market competition. Third, I have explained how a system of private profit-loss insurers would effectively minimize aggression, whether by private criminals or states, and promote a tendency toward civilization and perpetual peace. The only task outstanding, then, is to implement these insights: to withdraw one's consent and willing cooperation from the state and to promote its delegitimization in public opinion so as to persuade others to do the same. Without the erroneous public perception and judgment of the state as just and necessary and without the public's voluntary cooperation, even the seemingly most powerful government would implode and its powers evaporate. Thus liberated, we would regain our right to self-defense and be able to turn to freed and unregulated insurance agencies for efficient professional assistance in all matters of protection and conflict resolution.

References

Anderson, Terry, and P.J. Hill. 1979. "The American Experiment in Anarcho-Capitalism: The Not So Wild, Wild West." *Journal of Libertarian Studies* 3, no. 1.

Banfield, Edward C. 1974. *The Unheavenly City Revisited.* Boston: Little, Brown.

Benson, Bruce L. 1986. "Guns for Protection, and Other Private Sector Responses to the Government's Failure to Control Crime." *Journal of Libertarian Studies* 8, no. 1.

Boétie, Etienne de la. 1975. *The Politics of Obedience: The Discourse of Voluntary Servitude.* New York: Free Life Editions.

Buchanan, James M. 1975. *The Limits of Liberty.* Chicago: University of Chicago Press.

Buchanan, James M., and Gordon Tullock. 1962. *The Calculus of Consent.* Ann Arbor: University of Michigan Press.

Denson, John V., ed. 1997. *The Costs of War.* New Brunswick, N.J.: Transaction Publishers.

Fuller, John F.C. 1992. *The Conduct of War.* New York: Da Capo Press.

Hoppe, Hans-Hermann. 1993. *The Economics and Ethics of Private Property.* Boston: Kluwer.

——. 1998. "The Trouble With Classical Liberalism." *Rothbard-Rockwell Report* 9, no. 4.

——. 1997. "Where The Right Goes Wrong." *Rothbard-Rockwell Report* 8, no. 4.

——. 1997. "On Certainty and Uncertainty, Or: How Rational Can Our Expectations Be?" *Review of Austrian Economics* 10, no. 1.

———. 1997. "Time Preference, Government, and the Process of De-Civilization." *The Costs of War*. John V. Denson, ed. New Brunswick, N.J.: Transaction Publishers.

———. July 1995. "Free Immigration or Forced Integration?" *Chronicles*.

———. 1989. *A Theory of Socialism and Capitalism*. Boston: Kluwer.

Howard, Michael. 1976. *War in European History*. New York: Oxford University Press.

Hume, David. 1971. "The First Principles of Government." *Essays: Moral, Political, and Literary*. Oxford: Oxford University Press.

Knight, Frank H. 1971. *Risk, Uncertainty, and Profit*. Chicago: University of Chicago Press.

Krippendorff, Ekkehard. 1985. *Staat und Krieg*. Frankfurt/M.: Suhrkamp.

Kuehnelt-Leddihn, Erik von. 1990. *Leftism Revisited*. Washington, D.C.: Regnery.

Levin, Michael. 1997. *Why Race Matters*. Westport, Conn.: Praeger.

McGrath, Roger D. 1984. *Gunfighters, Highwaymen and Vigilantes: Violence on the Frontier*. Berkeley: University of California Press.

Mises, Ludwig von. 1981. *Socialism*. Indianapolis: Liberty Classics.

———. 1985. *Liberalism: In the Classical Tradition*. San Francisco: Cobden Press.

———. 1966. *Human Action*. Chicago: Regnery.

Mises, Richard von. 1957. *Probability, Statistics, and Truth*. New York: Dover.

Molinari, Gustave de. 1977. *The Production of Security*. New York: Center for Libertarian Studies.

Rothbard, Murray N. 1995. *The Logic of Action*, Vol. 2. *Applications and Criticism from the Austrian School*. Cheltenham, U.K.: Edward Elgar.

———. 1998. *The Ethics of Liberty*. New York: New York University Press.

———. 1993. *Man, Economy, and State*. Auburn, Ala.: Ludwig von Mises Institute.

———. 1978. *For A New Liberty*. New York: Collier.

———. 1977. *Power and Market*. Kansas City: Sheed Andrews and McMeel.

———. 1974. *Egalitarianism As A Revolt Against Nature and Other Essays*. Washington, D.C.: Libertarian Review Press.

Rushton, J. Philippe. 1995. *Race, Evolution, and Behavior*. New Brunswick, N.J.: Transaction Publishers.

Spooner, Lysander. 1966. *No Treason: The Constitution of No Authority*. Larkspur, Colo.: Pine Tree Press.

Tannehill, Morris and Linda. 1984. *The Market for Liberty*. New York: Laissez Faire Books.

Tilly, Charles. 1985. "War Making and State Making as Organized Crime." *Bringing the State Back In*. Peter B. Evans, Dietrich Rueschemeyer, Theda Skocpol, eds. Cambridge: Cambridge University Press.

Wilson, James Q., and Richard J. Herrnstein. 1985. *Crime and Human Nature*. New York: Simon and Schuster.

Printed in Great Britain
by Amazon